RACIAL INJUSTICE:
Rage, Protests, and Demands for Change

Hal Marcovitz

ReferencePoint Press

San Diego, CA

About the Author

Hal Marcovitz is a former newspaper reporter and columnist who has written more than two hundred books for young readers. He makes his home in Chalfont, Pennsylvania.

For more information, contact:
ReferencePoint Press, Inc.
PO Box 27779
San Diego, CA 92198
www.ReferencePointPress.com

Picture Credits:
Cover: Stephanie Kenner/Shutterstock

6: Drazen Zigic/Shutterstock
9: Michal Urbanek/Shutterstock
11: Maury Aaseng
16: Associated Press
22: Kevin Mohott/Reuters/Newscom

26: Hayk_Shalunts/Shutterstock
31: Aaron of LA Photography/Shutterstock
33: Associated Press
36: Ryan Garza/Zuma Press/Newscom
43: Associated Press
46: Associated Press
53: Bridgeman Images

LIBRARY OF CONGRESS CATALOGING-IN-PUBLICATION DATA

Names: Marcovitz, Hal, author.
Title: Racial injustice : rage, protests, and demands for change / by Hal Marcovitz.
Other titles: Rage, protests, and demands for change
Description: San Diego, CA : ReferencePoint Press, Inc., 2021. | Series: Being Black in America | Includes bibliographical references and index.
Identifiers: LCCN 2020041004 (print) | LCCN 2020041005 (ebook) | ISBN 9781678200282 (library binding) | ISBN 9781678200299 (ebook)
Subjects: LCSH: Black lives matter movement--Juvenile literature. | African Americans--Violence against--Juvenile literature. | Racial profiling in law enforcement--United States--Juvenile literature. | Civil rights movements--United States--History--21st century--Juvenile literature. | Floyd, George, 1973-2020--Juvenile literature. | African Americans--Social conditions--21st century--Juvenile literature. | Racism--United States--History--21st century--Juvenile literature. | United States--Race relations--History--21st century--Juvenile literature.
Classification: LCC E185.615 .M2873 2021 (print) | LCC E185.615 (ebook) | DDC 323.1196/073--dc23
LC record available at https://lccn.loc.gov/2020041004
LC ebook record available at https://lccn.loc.gov/2020041005

CONTENTS

The Chokehold

For nearly nine minutes, Minneapolis police officer Derek Chauvin pressed his knee into the neck of George Floyd, whose body was splayed upon a city street. Minutes earlier, Chauvin and three other officers had pulled Floyd out of his car and wrestled him to the street. The alleged crime that led to Floyd finding himself facing death on a Minneapolis street: Floyd, a forty-six-year-old Black man, was suspected of using a counterfeit twenty-dollar bill to pay for a pack of cigarettes at a nearby convenience store.

Floyd's arrest on the night of May 25, 2020, was captured on cell phone video by a witness. As he struggled under the pressure of Chauvin's knee, it was clear that Floyd was in terrible distress. The video recorded Floyd's last words before he lost consciousness: "Man, I can't breathe."[1] The maneuver applied to Floyd—known as the chokehold—proved fatal.

An autopsy performed on Floyd's body indicated that he lost consciousness more than a minute before Chauvin finally released his knee. When ambulance crew members arrived minutes later, they were unable to revive Floyd. Efforts to revive Floyd in the ambulance and at a nearby hospital proved futile, and he was declared dead.

Controversial Tactic

In subduing Floyd, Chauvin employed a controversial tactic that has been used for decades by many police officers to detain criminal suspects. The chokehold is used to cut off air to the suspect's lungs, causing the suspect to lose consciousness. Police officers often apply chokeholds by wrapping their arms around a suspect's neck, but other maneuvers are applied as well. In Floyd's case, Chauvin applied the chokehold by kneeling on Floyd's neck. The chokehold is not a tactic that is universally employed by all police departments. Starting in the 1980s, physicians looked at the chokehold and found it to be excessively dangerous, often resulting in death. A 1982 study written by physicians Donald T. Reay and John W. Eisele reported that it should only be applied in cases in which the arresting officer believes his or her life is at risk. "No officer should be lulled into the false confidence that squeezing an arm about the neck is a safe and innocuous technique of subduing a suspect," reported the study. "It must be viewed as a potentially fatal tactic and reserved to situations which merit its risk."[2]

> "No officer should be lulled into the false confidence that squeezing an arm about the neck is a safe and innocuous technique of subduing a suspect."[2]
>
> —Physicians Donald T. Reay and John W. Eisele

Based on the events seen in the cell phone video, neither Chauvin nor the three other officers who participated in the arrest—including two who helped pin Floyd's body to the street—appeared to be in danger when Chauvin knelt on Floyd's neck. In fact, since the Reay-Eisele study and others done around the same time, numerous police departments had already banned the tactic from use among their officers. Nevertheless, a 2013 study by the US Department of Justice found that among American police departments serving populations of 1 million or more citizens, 43 percent of those departments continued to permit their officers to subdue criminal suspects by using chokeholds.

Protests Against Racial Injustice

The video showing Chauvin pressing his knee into Floyd's neck was soon uploaded to social media. Within hours, massive protests against racial injustice against Black Americans erupted on the streets of Minneapolis. Within days, those protests spread to numerous other cities, small towns, and suburban communities across America.

The killing of Floyd wasn't the only example of racial injustice raised by the protesters. They were quick to point out that Black Americans have been victims of racial injustice for decades if not centuries. Meanwhile, on the streets of Minneapolis and other communities, the words "I can't breathe" became a ral-

The death of George Floyd at the hands of police sparked immediate protests in Minneapolis and across the nation. Many who took to the streets were angered not only by Floyd's death but by a history of perceived law-enforcement bias against people of color.

lying cry for change. Floyd's final words were shouted by thousands of demonstrators who spent the long and uneasy summer of 2020 demanding justice for Floyd and other Black Americans who were the victims of police abuse.

The video showing Floyd's last desperate moments of life likely had a lot to do with the impassioned response. Says Black journalist Eileen Rivers:

George Floyd . . . was handcuffed and pinned down by Minneapolis cops. One officer pressed his knee into Floyd's neck for several minutes as three others stood by. Floyd said he couldn't breathe. Then he died. . . . It makes me fear for my brother who lives in Colorado and can, at times, be a bit of a hothead. It also makes me fear for my brother in California, whose temper is a bit more laid back. It takes a lot to really get him angry. I fear for him because I know that it doesn't take a Black man being angry to get killed by a cop. It just takes a Black man being Black.[3]

Ultimately, millions of Americans viewed the video of Chauvin kneeling on Floyd's neck on social media or on national newscasts. That ugly scene of Floyd pleading for his life sparked a national wave of protests that caused many Americans to question whether their nation truly does guarantee equal justice for all.

CHAPTER ONE

Enduring Decades of Injustice

For much of the first half of 2020, Tanya Faison left home as little as possible. Due to a respiratory condition, Faison did not want to risk exposure to COVID-19, which by the end of May had already claimed more than one hundred thousand American lives. But then news of George Floyd's death emerged out of Minneapolis, and Faison decided that she could stay home no longer. She donned a protective mask and joined other protesters in her home city of Sacramento, California, to demand an end to racial injustice. "There comes a time when you need to figure out what's more of a risk," she said. "So I'm going to put my mask on, I'm going to put my gloves on, and I'm going to protest."[4]

> "I'm going to put my mask on, I'm going to put my gloves on, and I'm going to protest."[4]
>
> —Tanya Faison, president of the Sacramento, California, chapter of Black Lives Matter

Faison is president of the Sacramento chapter of Black Lives Matter, the national civil rights group that formed following the death of eighteen-year-old Michael Brown. Brown, an African American, was fatally shot during a confrontation with police in 2014 in Ferguson, Missouri. As with the case of Floyd, Brown had been accused of committing a minor crime—shoplifting a package of cigars—when the Ferguson police officer resorted to deadly force to subdue him.

Brown and Floyd are just two of the Black Americans who have been killed by police in recent years. These deaths have marked a turning point in the long struggle for equality for African Americans. Many do not believe they enjoy the rights of full citizenship, not only in the criminal justice system but in many facets of American life, including housing, education, and access to medical care. Many Black Americans have found that after years of calling for change and relying on mostly White political leaders to enact laws and policies guaranteeing equality, they now have no other recourse than to take their protests into the streets. "This isn't just about George Floyd," says Yvonne Passmore, a Black resident of Minneapolis. "This is about

Despite the deadly COVID-19 pandemic, large numbers of young Americans gathered for the Black Lives Matter protests that surged in the nation's cities. Many wore masks and other protective gear to stay safe while marching and speaking out against racism.

years and years of being treated as less than people—and not just by police. It's everything. We don't get proper medical. We don't get proper housing. There's so much discrimination, and it's not just the justice system. It's a whole lot of things."[5]

Few Easy Paths for Blacks

As Passmore says, for decades Black Americans have suffered indignities across many facets of American life. Many Blacks have been confronted by police officers or security guards because White store employees feared they would commit thefts. This trend is known as retail racism. Workplaces are often unfriendly to Black Americans as well. Black employees have often found that many avenues of advancement are closed to them. A 2019 study by the National Opinion Research Center (NORC) at the University of Chicago found that while Blacks annually make up 10 percent of all college graduates, few of them have found easy paths toward senior management jobs at major US corporations. The study found that Blacks hold just 3.8 percent of senior management jobs in the nation's five hundred largest corporations.

Black Americans find hostility on high school and college campuses too. Regarded by many as centers of progressive ideas, schools have nevertheless often been the scenes of ugly racism. In 2020, for example, students who walked into a campus gift shop at Michigan State University were shocked to see a display of Black dolls hanging from a toy tree—as though they had been lynched in the post–Civil War South. The dolls resembled famous figures, among them former president Barack Obama. After Black students complained, the dolls were removed from the store display. Says Black journalist Adrienne Green, "Resilience has long been glorified as integral to being a successful student. But research has shown that the higher-education experience often requires that black students employ even more grit than their white peers if they want to achieve both in the classroom and outside of it, where they have to overcome [stereotyping] and straight-up racism."[6]

While ugly examples of racism are hurtful, the attitudes and routine practices of many police departments too often cost African Americans their dignity—and their lives. According to data collected by the *Washington Post*, 5,033 Americans died in police shootings from 2015 through 2020. Of those deaths, 1,329 (or about 26 percent) were Black. That is a high percentage, given that Blacks compose just 13 percent of the US population.

Black Americans Experience Higher Rate of Police Killings than White Americans

Police kill Black Americans at a much higher rate than White Americans, according to data collected by the *Washington Post* between 2015 and 2020. Actual numbers show that more Whites were killed by police during that period (2,573) than Blacks (1,335). But Blacks make up less than 13 percent of the US population compared with Whites, who make up 60 percent. Based on their numbers in the population, African Americans are being killed at a disproportionate rate of 32 per million versus 13 per million for Whites. The data also show a disproportionate rate of Hispanics killed by police.

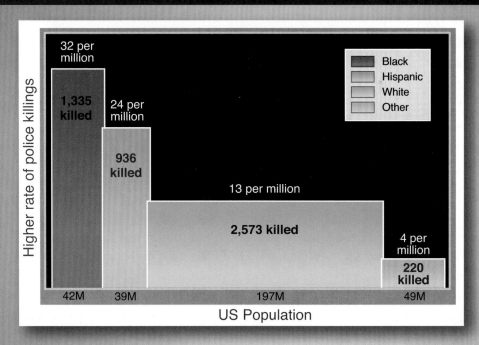

Source: "Fatal Force," *Washington Post*, September 8, 2020.
https://www.washingtonpost.com/graphics/investigations/police-shootings-database/.

Another organization, Mapping Police Violence, looked at police shootings in 2018 in large cities, most of which have large numbers of Black residents. The numbers are disturbing. In the one hundred largest US cities, the group found, African Americans accounted for 38 percent of the victims of police shootings, even though they represented just 21 percent of the populations in those cities.

These and other statistics reveal that in the nation's largest cities, Black people are nearly twice as likely to die in police shootings as White people. A 2019 article in the scientific journal *Nature* comments on this dynamic: "The results paint a picture of definite disparity when it comes to race and police shootings. Although more white people are shot in total, people from minority ethnic groups are shot at higher rates by population."[7] Moreover, a 2019 study published in the journal *Proceedings of the National Academy of Sciences* found that a Black man is 2.5 times more likely than a White man to be killed by police during his lifetime. Write the authors of the study, "For young men of color, police use of force is among the leading causes of death."[8] The study found that at least one out of every one thousand Black men in America is likely to die in a police shooting.

Why Do Police Target Blacks?

Racist attitudes toward Blacks are not a recent development in the culture of American police. These attitudes date back to the years before the Civil War. During that time, police officers in the South—who in many cases were volunteers serving without pay—were charged with tracking down escaped slaves as well as suppressing slave rebellions against White plantation owners. Tactics practiced by the so-called slave patrols could be brutal, often resulting in the torture or murder of the slaves. Following the Civil War the slave patrols were abolished, and professional police forces were established. But laws biased against Blacks, known as Jim Crow laws, adopted in the Southern states denied freed Blacks many of the rights guaranteed to White Americans—and professional police forces were charged with enforcing those laws.

Why Many Black Americans Will Not Call the Police

Many African Americans say they are fearful of calling police even when they are victims of a crime. Journalist Nikole Hannah-Jones explains why this is so. She describes an incident that took place in 2014. She was walking with friends and family members along a crowded beach on Long Island, New York, when a young man fired a gun nearby. The young man fled and disappeared down a nearby street. No one had been hurt. Says Hannah-Jones:

> My friends and I locked eyes in stunned silence. Between the four adults, we hold six degrees. Three of us are journalists. And not one of us had thought to call the police. We had not even considered it.
>
> We also are all black. . . . Calling the police posed considerable risks. It carried the very real possibility of inviting disrespect, even physical harm. We had seen witnesses treated like suspects, and knew how quickly black people calling the police for help could wind up cuffed in the back of a squad car. Some of us knew of black professionals who'd had guns drawn on them for no reason.

Nikole Hannah-Jones, "Yes, Black America Fears the Police. Here's Why," ProPublica, March 4, 2015. www.propublica.org.

By the 1960s the Jim Crow laws had been abolished, but the targeting of Blacks continued in the South—and occurred in the northern states as well. An example of this could be seen in President Richard Nixon's national campaign to end the illegal drug trade. Begun in 1971, this effort mostly targeted low-level drug dealers in urban Black neighborhoods. "We could arrest their leaders, raid their homes, break up their meetings, and vilify them night after night on the evening news,"[9] John Ehrlichman, one of Nixon's chief advisers, said in a 1994 interview with *Harper's Magazine*. Yet again, police charged with enforcing the laws were mostly targeting African Americans.

Although racist attitudes are not universal in law enforcement, activists say they persist in many police departments. This culture of bias toward African Americans, they contend, is often passed down from veteran officers to new recruits. Derek Chauvin, the police officer who pressed his knee into Floyd's neck, was a nineteen-year veteran of the Minneapolis Police Department. His duties included training young officers. In fact, the three officers who assisted Chauvin in Floyd's arrest were all young officers who had recently joined the Minneapolis police force. "[Veteran officers] pass on that socialization of 'I don't care what you learned in the academy; this is how you do it on the street,'"[10] says Ryan Getty, a former police officer who is now a criminologist at California State University, Sacramento.

Black Women Fear the Police

Fear of how they will be treated by police has had a dramatic impact on the way many Black Americans live their lives. Many Black parents have what is known as "the Talk" with their sons when they are young. They explain what to do in the event their sons are stopped and questioned by police. Says Kenya Young, a Black mother of three boys, "I remember the kids asking to go to the park and the laundry list of what I had to tell them: 'Don't wear your hood. Don't put your hands in your pocket. If you get stopped, don't run. Put your hands up. Don't make a lot of moves. . . . I mean, it just went on and on."[11]

While young Black men have always had much to fear from police, in recent years young Black women have learned they have much to fear as well. Although the deaths of Black men frequently dominate the headlines, there have been cases in which Black women and girls have also been victimized. Among them are Rekia Boyd, a twenty-two-year-old Chicago woman fatally shot by an off-duty police officer during an altercation in 2012 in a public park; Tarika Wilson, a twenty-six-year-old mother who was fatally shot by police in 2008 in Lima, Ohio, while holding her year-old son in her arms; Aiyana Jones, a seven-year-old girl who was fatally shot during a 2010 police raid in Detroit, Michigan; and Miriam Carey, a thirty-four-year-old dental hygienist, whose inadvertent wrong turn onto the White House grounds in Washington, DC, in 2013 led to a police chase and her death by gunshots fired by police.

Andrea J. Ritchie, an author and Black activist, believes many White police officers feel threatened when they confront Black women, who may respond with angry protests against their treatment by the White officers. Such confrontations escalate into violence, she argues, because "Black women's mere presence, speech, and protest of mistreatment . . . [are] a threat that officers meet with physical or even deadly force."[12]

The 2020 shooting death of Breonna Taylor has drawn the most attention to the plight of Black women. Taylor, a twenty-six-year-old emergency medical technician, and her boyfriend, Kenneth Walker, were in bed in her Louisville, Kentucky, apartment on the night of March 13 when they heard a loud banging on the door. Walker said they asked who was there but then suddenly, without identifying themselves, three police officers burst into the apartment. The police suspected, wrongly, that a drug dealer was using the apartment to sell narcotics. The officers, who have said they did identify themselves, crashed through Taylor's door with guns drawn. Believing their lives to be in danger, Taylor's boyfriend grabbed his gun and fired at the intruders. The police officers returned fire, spraying the apartment with bullets. Taylor was struck with a fatal shot. Her death has also become a rallying point for the 2020 protests. Says journalist Arwa Mahdawi, "Black women are rarely centered in narratives about police violence; they are rarely the catalysts for mass outrage; their deaths are often an afterthought. Which is why we must keep fighting for justice for Breonna Taylor; we must keep saying her name."[13]

The fatal shooting of Breonna Taylor by Louisville police became another rallying point of the 2020 Black Lives Matter movement. Mourners built makeshift shrines and shouted "Say Her Name" to remind the country of recurring incidents of police violence against Black women.

The Birth of Black Lives Matter

In many ways the recent protests are an extension of the anger, grief, and frustration that erupted following the 2014 death of Brown in Ferguson. Emerging from those earlier protests was the establishment of the Black Lives Matter movement. In previous years police violence against Black citizens had resulted in protests, but these activities were often restricted to protesters registering their complaints on social media. However, the Brown case prompted protesters to take the next step—from complaining about the treatment of Blacks on their Twitter and Instagram accounts to actually taking to the streets and demanding substantial change.

Wesley Lowery, a Black journalist, was assigned by his newspaper, the *Washington Post*, to cover the demonstrations in Ferguson and other cities in the aftermath of Brown's death. He saw the Black Lives Matter movement materialize on the streets of Ferguson as protesters demanded that their voices be heard. He writes:

What happened in Ferguson would give birth to a movement and set the nation on course for an ongoing public hearing on race that stretched far past the killing of unarmed residents. . . . The social justice movement spawned from Mike Brown's blood would force city after city to grapple with its own fraught histories of race and policing. As protests propelled by tweets and hashtags spread under the banner of Black Lives Matter and with mobile phone and body camera video shining new light on the way police interact with minority communities, America was forced to consider that not everyone marching in the streets could be wrong.[14]

Stark Images of Brown's Body

The slogan "Black Lives Matter" was actually used for the first time a year before Brown's death. It was conceived by Black activist Alicia Garza of Oakland, California. Along with millions of other Americans, Garza was shocked when a jury acquitted George Zimmerman, a Florida neighborhood watch volunteer, in the 2012 shooting death of Black teenager Trayvon Martin. Martin was walking home after buying a bag of candy and an iced tea at a nearby convenience store when he encountered the patrolling Zimmerman, scuffled with him, and was shot and killed by Zimmerman. Zimmerman told police he suspected Martin of planning a burglary in the community. In a Facebook post following Zimmerman's acquittal, Garza said:

> "The social justice movement spawned from Mike Brown's blood would force city after city to grapple with its own fraught histories of race and policing."[14]
>
> —Black journalist Wesley Lowery

The sad part is, there's a section of America who is cheering and celebrating right now, and that makes me sick to my stomach. We GOTTA get it together y'all. Stop saying we are not surprised. That's a damn shame in itself.

I continue to be surprised at how little Black lives matter. And I will continue that. Stop giving up on Black life. Black people. I love you. I love us. Our lives matter.[15]

Others responded. Activist Patrisse Cullors saw Garza's Facebook post and reposted the slogan "Black Lives Matter." Soon a third activist, Opal Tometi, established a Twitter account under the slogan. By 2020 the Black Lives Matter Twitter account reported nearly 950,000 followers.

> "Stop giving up on Black life. Black people. I love you. I love us. Our lives matter."[15]
>
> —Black activist Alicia Garza

Activists say it was the stark images of Brown's body left lying in the street—medical examiners did not collect the body for four hours after the shooting—that prompted them to take the next step. They moved their protests off social media and onto the streets of Ferguson and other communities. "The delay helped fuel the outrage," says Patricia Bynes, an African American political leader in Ferguson. "It was very disrespectful to the community and the people who live there. It also sent the message from law enforcement that 'we can do this to you any day, any time, in broad daylight, and there's nothing you can do about it.'"[16]

Moreover, the outrage was further fueled when prosecutors investigating Brown's death announced in November 2014 that they found no reason to criminally charge Darren Wilson, the White Ferguson officer who fired the fatal shot at Brown. Hours after prosecutors announced that Wilson would not face charges, angry protests again broke out in the streets of Ferguson as well as other cities. "The system failed us again,"[17] said one Black woman who protested in the streets of Ferguson.

Brown's death had spawned the Black Lives Matter movement, but few of the changes demanded by protesters then had been accomplished by 2020. That is why Floyd died as a police

The No-Knock Warrant

Breonna Taylor sustained a fatal gunshot wound as police crashed through her apartment door in the mistaken belief that the apartment was a center of drug trafficking. But police cannot just enter a home without authorization from a judge. They must first obtain a search warrant, proving to the judge that they have probable cause to suspect the residence is the scene of a crime. In Taylor's case police obtained what is known as a "no-knock warrant," meaning the search warrant gave them permission to enter the home without first announcing why they were there.

No-knock warrants were first used during President Richard Nixon's war on drugs, which, starting in 1971, spent hundreds of millions of dollars to stamp out the illegal drug trade—mostly targeting low-level dealers in urban Black neighborhoods. Says author Radley Balko, "It was this idea of just showing, you know, how tough we were on crime and drugs by letting cops just sort of kick down doors without announcing themselves first. . . . It became sort of widespread—really widespread in the 1980s in police departments across the country as we kind of, you know, really militarized and ramped up the war on drugs."

Quoted in Mary Louise Kelly, "No-Knock Warrants: How Common They Are and Why Police Are Using Them," *All Things Considered*, National Public Radio, June 12, 2020. www.npr.org.

officer forced a knee into his neck and why Taylor was killed in a hail of gunfire. In fact, according to Mapping Police Violence, in the four-month period following the death of Floyd, another 305 Americans were killed in police shootings. Among them were fifty-four Black Americans. This number represented 18 percent of the total—again a number reflecting a higher proportion than the 13 percent of Americans who are Black. In other words, police violence against Black Americans has continued despite massive protests in the streets denouncing such behavior. The Black Lives Matter movement has accomplished a lot in calling attention to the plight of Black Americans, but the deaths of Floyd, Taylor, and others show that America still has a long way to go.

CHAPTER TWO

Protests Sweep Across America

George Floyd's funeral was scheduled for June 9, 2020, in Houston, Texas, the city where he grew up. A week before the funeral, a massive demonstration was staged on the streets of Houston to call attention to racial inequality and police abuse. The rally was organized by two of Floyd's childhood friends, Frazier Thompson III and Bernard Freeman. Both men had become successful hip hop stars, Thompson rapping under the name of Trae tha Truth while Freeman was known as Bun B. "I want to make George and his family proud," said Thompson. "We're going to show the nation how we stand together and stand up in Houston, Texas."[18]

The protest was scheduled to begin at a downtown Houston park known as Discovery Green. From the park, protesters planned to march twelve blocks through city streets, ending at Houston City Hall, where Thompson and Freeman as well as leaders of the Black Lives Matter movement and sympathetic political leaders planned to address the crowd. More than sixty thousand protesters swarmed into the streets of Houston that day. So many people showed up for the event that many of the protesters could not get close enough to the city hall to hear the speeches. Moreover, many of the protesters remained in the streets well into the night, hours after the speeches ended.

One of the protesters, Brison Gresham, wore a T-shirt that read, "I Hope I Don't Get Killed For Being Black Today." He said, "I'm feeling mad, I'm feeling sad, also confused at the same time. Like I don't really understand why people got to treat us this way."[19]

> "We're going to show the nation how we stand together and stand up in Houston, Texas."[18]
>
> —Hip hop star Trae tha Truth, aka Frazier Thompson III

Peaceful Protest

In the days following Floyd's death, protests erupted on streets throughout American cities, small towns, and suburban communities. Many of them were similar to the protest staged in Houston that day—marches conducted on the streets to protest the deaths of Floyd as well as Breonna Taylor and other victims of racial injustice. During his speech in front of Houston City Hall, Freeman called for Black Americans as well as others who support their cause to run for election and win seats in city councils, state legislatures, and the US Congress so that new laws could be adopted, ensuring equal treatment for African Americans. "We want to start here," he said. "We want Houston to be able to send out a message that we won't stand for injustice, we won't stand for police brutality and so we know that there are different policy reforms that could take place to help improve this situation in our city."[20]

The June 2 demonstration in Houston was largely peaceful. "The people who knew George the best help set the tone for Houston. They knew what he was about. He truly was a gentle giant, a sweet guy,"[21] said the Reverend David Hill, a Houston community activist and local pastor who knows the Floyd family.

Still, as the protest progressed, police stood by, watching for signs of trouble. There were moments in which tempers flared. Some protesters angrily threw trash or water bottles at the police officers lining the route. Other protesters quickly stepped in and hustled them away, pulling them into the crowd where

A man wears an "I Hope I Don't Get Killed For Being Black Today" T-shirt during a BLM protest. The slogan garnered some media attention when University of Houston basketball player Brison Gresham donned one of these shirts while attending a Houston rally in remembrance of George Floyd.

their tempers could ease. A few dozen arrests were made that day for disorderly conduct. Overall, though, leaders of the event said they felt they had gotten their message across in a day dedicated to peaceful protest and a call for change. "We are not trying to see our city torn up," said protester Ronnie Daniel. "My city is all I have. My black people are all I have. I'm all I have."[22]

All Races Join the Protests

As Americans watched TV news coverage of the protests in Houston and other cities, they witnessed a remarkable sight. In this age of deeply polarized attitudes on nearly every imaginable topic, the protesters included many African Americans but also an unmistakable mix of races, ages, and genders.

Many of the protesters who have joined Black citizens in the streets are members of younger generations—Americans born since the 1980s. Black Lives Matter cofounder Alicia Garza says she has seen a growing dissatisfaction among young people about the way older generations and their political leaders have tackled many issues, among them gun violence and climate change. Garza says young activists have been very vocal on those issues, so it is not shocking to see young people also take on the issue of racial injustice. Cherish Patton, an eighteen-year-old Black Lives Matter leader who organized several demonstrations in New York City, says, "We see so many white people who hate us, absolutely hate us for the way that we look. To see white people on the front lines, it's exciting to know that these younger generations of white people care."[23]

Patton formerly attended high school in New York City with Michelle Moran, a White student who often took positions in class defending White political leaders and others in authority. But even before Floyd's death, Moran had changed her thinking and come to realize that Black citizens are often the victims of racial injustice. "I slowly but surely opened my eyes to the horrors of the criminal justice system,"[24] says Moran. After Floyd's death, Moran participated in a number of demonstrations organized by Patton and other Black activists in New York.

Teens and young adults, who stood out because of their numbers in many of the protests, were joined by people of varying ages. Mary Carrigan Holden, a sixty-eight-year-old White woman and retired teacher, was arrested for criminal trespass in August 2020 in Louisville, Kentucky. Holden was one of about a dozen senior citizens in Louisville who participated in a protest demanding the arrest of the police officers who broke into Breonna Taylor's apartment. The protesters carried signs that read "Grannies for Breonna," and "Listen to Your Elders, Black Lives Matter." Holden was arrested after she crossed over from the street onto the front lawn of the home of Kentucky attorney general Daniel Cameron. Protesters had gathered in front of Cameron's home to call on him to prosecute the police officers.

> "The murder of George Floyd obviously sparked something in White people that made them realize we need to get involved now."[25]
>
> —Thousand Oaks, California, community organizer Jon Cummings

Holden said she understood that at the age of sixty-eight she was risking her health should she be exposed to COVID-19 during the chaotic protest. (During the pandemic, senior citizens were regarded as most susceptible to the deadly effects of the virus.) Still, she said, it was a risk worth taking. "I took a risk today because sometimes ideals are more important than health,"[25] Holden said.

Vandalism and Looting

Many of the protests around the country were largely peaceful. Although tempers occasionally flared and minor scuffles did break out, many protesters focused their energies on the purpose of the demonstrations: calling attention to racial injustice through speeches and marching.

But this was not the case everywhere. In many cities, the protests exploded into scenes that were never envisioned by the organizers. Vandals smashed store and car windows along protest routes. They slashed tires. They looted businesses. They burned buildings and cars.

Protests that broke out in Philadelphia on May 31 resulted in nearly one hundred arrests. About half of the people arrested in the city that day were charged with looting. Most of the other

Black Lives Matter in Europe

As protests against racial injustice swept across America, many European countries faced the reality that many of their Black citizens also do not feel they enjoy equal treatment. In fact, protests against racial injustice were staged in several European nations. In France, for example, protesters gathered on June 13, 2020, at the Place de la République, a central square in the city of Paris. "The death of George Floyd has a strong echo in the death in France of my little brother," said Assa Traoré, whose twenty-four-year-old brother, Adama Traoré, died near Paris in 2016 after police detained him. "What's happening in the United States is happening in France. Our brothers are dying."

Meanwhile, in London, England, thousands of protesters marched through several city neighborhoods. "I feel that what happened in the US was just a spark, that sparked everywhere. . . . I do think George Floyd's death sparked it across the world and I think it's amazing," said one protester taking part in a June 8 demonstration in London. Said another protester, "It's a worldwide issue, no matter where you are. It's an issue everywhere, we all need to rise up."

Quoted in Reuters, "Black Lives Matter Protests Turn Violent Across Europe," Voice of America, June 13, 2020. www .voanews.com.

Quoted in Rob Picheta et al., "Thousands Join Black Lives Matter Protest in London, as Bolted Police Horse Causes Panic," CNN, June 8, 2020. www.cnn.com.

arrests were for disorderly conduct. During protests staged in the city the following day, several buildings were set on fire. The mayhem became so widespread that during the second day of protests, Mayor James Kenney enacted a 6 p.m. curfew—ordering all people off the streets until 6 a.m. the following morning.

Philadelphia district attorney Larry Krasner said that people with little interest in the protests had merged into the crowds with the specific intent of looting businesses along the protest routes. "They don't seem to be carrying signs, talking about political issues or talking about police accountability," Krasner said.

"They don't seem to have T-shirts on that are political in nature. They seem to be committing opportunistic crimes and they seem to be doing it within the context of peaceful protest."[26]

Philadelphia police commissioner Danielle Outlaw, an African American, said she understands the frustration felt by Black citizens and supports their right to carry out peaceful protests in the streets. "Throughout the nation, communities of color are tired of reliving atrocities such as this over and over again. They are sick and tired of being sick and tired,"[27] Outlaw said. But she is also angered when she sees people with no interest at all in curing

Several individuals who joined the Black Lives Matter crowds set out to vandalize and destroy property. Some looted, others set fires. This behavior prompted some city officials and media commentators to criticize the largely peaceful protests for inciting violence.

racial injustice use peaceful protests as opportunities to commit crimes and steal from innocent store owners. She said,

> To hold up a Black Lives Matter sign and then use the destruction that they were committing in the name of Black Lives Matter is not only a slap in the face, but it's completely a setback for everything that's been accomplished by those who have been working to improve civil rights over many decades, and those who are working internally to do our parts to fix the issues within the criminal justice system.[28]

In the days following the protests in Philadelphia, many downtown city streets were left in shambles. Broken glass littered sidewalks and streets. Trash was strewn across neighborhoods. Plywood sheets had replaced doors and windows in dozens of businesses that had been vandalized and looted. Soon, though, neighbors filled the streets to take on the chore of cleaning up after the vandals and looters. Said one Philadelphia woman as she knelt and stuffed loose papers into a trash bag, "I thought, 'This is my neighborhood, I have to clean up. This is the right thing to do.'"[29]

Protesting in Small Towns

For several weeks during the spring and summer of 2020, it seemed as though protests were taking place all across America—and not just in big cities. Even in small towns and suburban communities—many with very small populations of Black citizens—residents turned out to protest racial injustice and police killings.

One of these small communities was Souderton, a suburban Pennsylvania community of about sixty-seven hundred located about 25 miles (40 km) north of Philadelphia. The town employs just a dozen police officers—and many of them are on a first-name basis with the citizens they serve. On June 5 several hundred residents of Souderton, most of whom were

Protesting Bias by Campus Police

One demonstration demanding racial justice staged in July 2020 occurred on the campus of Temple University in Philadelphia. About one hundred students protested how Black students are treated by campus police. Many Black students complained that they have been racially profiled by campus police—stopped and questioned by police and asked to show their student identification cards while walking across campus.

Other college campuses have seen similar demonstrations. In October 2019 about 120 students and faculty members staged a protest at American University in Washington, DC, after a Black student, Gianna Wheeler, was suspended from the school after she was wrongly accused of assaulting another student. A half-dozen campus police officers dragged Wheeler out of her dormitory room, then barred her from returning to the campus. Wheeler was later found innocent of the charge by a university board appointed to investigate the case. "It was so outrageous that anybody would be treated like that," says Adrienne Pine, an anthropology professor who took part in the protest. "As far as I'm concerned, there is nothing that justifies the way that she was treated by those police."

Quoted in Elin Johnson, "Forced Removal of Student Prompts Protest," *Inside Higher Ed*, October 31, 2019. www.insidehighered.com.

White, marched down Broad Street in the small town to protest against racial injustice.

The protest was organized by Veronica Moeller, an African American college student who spent her whole life in Souderton. Says Moeller:

> Growing up black in Souderton, I actually lived a very, very privileged life. I never thought twice about my blackness or that being a thing. . . . This past week, not only for me,

but for my community, has been extremely difficult. I have cried so much thinking about my family and how one day I will have to prepare my daughter for how hateful this country can be just because she has brown skin.[30]

Among the marchers that day were several White political leaders, including Souderton mayor John Reynolds. He said, "As we watched the news of George Floyd last week, as he called out, 'I can't breathe,' we could see plainly that something is seriously wrong, especially for our citizens of color. Our society has not worked for them, but against them."[31]

Public Opinion Supports the Movement

Weeks after the death of Floyd, hundreds of protests against racial injustice had been staged in communities large and small. News coverage that had previously focused almost exclusively on the pain, struggles, and politics of the COVID-19 pandemic now brought vivid images of police killings of Black Americans and the massive protests into people's homes. These images brought about an awakening of sorts. According to a July 2020 national Gallup poll, 65 percent of American adults agreed with the message of the protesters: that racial injustice is a serious problem in American life and needs to be addressed. Moreover, 54 percent of the respondents said that the protests helped change their views on the issue, convincing them that police officers often abuse Black citizens—a notion they did not share prior to the protests.

Among the people who found themselves in agreement with the polling data was John Collins, a sixty-three-year-old White

> "As we watched the news of George Floyd last week, as he called out, 'I can't breathe,' we could see plainly that something is seriously wrong, especially for our citizens of color."[31]
>
> —Souderton, Pennsylvania, mayor John Reynolds

resident of central Florida. Due to the COVID-19 pandemic, Collins was furloughed from his job. Forced to stay home all summer, Collins watched TV news coverage of the demonstrations and quickly sympathized with the protesters as well as Black citizens who have been abused by the police. "The more you see it the more it boils inside," says Collins. "And I guess the boiling inside just kind of said, 'What can you do?'"[32]

Collins decided not to join protest marches, but he still took action. He wrote letters to his US representative and senators in Washington, demanding that they enact laws to eliminate racial injustice. He never heard back from those elected officials, but Collins says he knows it is important for constituents to press members of Congress to act on the issue.

Back the Blue Rallies

Not all Americans reacted as Collins did. Many rallied in support of police, holding counterprotests known as Back the Blue rallies. (Blue is the most familiar color found in American police uniforms.)

On July 25, for example, more than one thousand people held a rally in Eisenhower Park in East Meadow, New York. Many police officers from nearby New York City as well as several suburban departments attended the demonstration along with their supporters. One of the speakers at the demonstration was Genesis Familia, a Black woman who lost her mother, New York City police detective Miosotis Familia, in 2017 when she was killed by a shooter while sitting in a squad car in the city's Bronx borough. "[Miosotis] was an amazing human being and she was taken from me and those that loved her and that knew her for the blue uniform that she proudly wore," Genesis says. "And I just want all

> "I just want all Americans to remember that all these cops out here protecting us are human beings with families and friends and loved ones who need them to come home."[33]
>
> —Genesis Familia, a Black woman and the daughter of slain New York City police detective Miosotis Familia

Americans to remember that all these cops out here protecting us are human beings with families and friends and loved ones who need them to come home."[33]

While it is clear that many Americans continue to support their local police departments, the wide-scale protests that were staged in hundreds of American communities during the summer of 2020 showed that Americans of all races no longer accept systemic racism as the norm. They no longer accept the use of excessive force by police against unarmed Black citizens. Polls taken by Gallup and other groups show that many Americans— whether they are young people like Cherish Patton and Michelle Moran or older adults like Mary Carrigan Holden—do not view racial injustice as an acceptable part of American culture. And the unrest of the summer of 2020 suggests that the protests are likely to continue until real changes take place.

CHAPTER THREE

Governments Respond to the Protests

As was common in many cities, in the hours following the death of George Floyd, protesters flooded into the streets of Denver, Colorado, to demand justice and racial equality. For several nights the protests turned violent as stores and vehicles were vandalized. Police were called in to quell the demonstrations; they arrested many protesters. On May 30 Denver mayor Michael Hancock, an African American, enacted an 8:00 p.m. curfew to keep protesters off the streets after dark.

On June 3, though, protest leaders approached Hancock and said they planned to stage a rally that evening on the grounds of the Colorado State Capitol, which is located in Denver. They invited Hancock to join them, and he agreed. (By then, most of Denver's citizens had spent a quiet weekend at home, and Hancock had permitted his curfew order to expire.)

The event commenced as the rally participants lay down on their stomachs, their hands clasped behind their backs, to show their sympathy with Floyd's predicament shortly before his death. The protest then moved to the nearby Greek Amphitheatre, a public square in Denver. Several speakers addressed thousands of protesters gathered in the square. One of the speakers was the Denver mayor. "This is an amazing, peaceful, successful demonstration of raising the voices around freedom and justice and togetherness," Hancock said. "I'm proud of the demonstrations going on here tonight."[34]

The Denver police have often been accused of abusing Black citizens. On May 7, 2020, just weeks before the death of Floyd, Denver police officers handcuffed a Black man, Naphtali Israel, after they wrongly suspected him of brandishing a gun in a supermarket parking lot. During the incident, the police officers pointed their guns at Israel as well as at his car, where his wife and three daughters were sitting. After questioning in the parking lot, Israel was released. Moreover, an investigation by

> "This is an amazing, peaceful, successful demonstration of raising the voices around freedom and justice and togetherness."[34]
>
> —Denver, Colorado, mayor Michael Hancock

Denver mayor Michael Hancock was one of a few civic leaders who joined protesters in peacefully assembling and airing their complaints against racial bias in law enforcement. He promised that the city's police would strive to become more sensitive to race issues.

the Denver internet news site, Westword.com, unearthed thirty-eight cases of police abuse against Black citizens by the city's police since 2004.

Hancock promised the crowd that the city government would find ways to make its police force more racially sensitive. Even as he spoke, leaders of the city's police department were holding a virtual town hall to solicit comments from citizens on ways to improve relations with the Black community. (The town hall was held online because of the COVID-19 pandemic.) During the town hall, Denver citizens called on police to seek guidance from Black civil rights leaders in the city and to announce specific steps they would take against officers if they are found to have abused Black citizens. After listening to the comments, Police Chief Paul Pazen said, "We have to do a better job of identifying

The Right to Protest

The right to protest is regarded as an exercise of free speech and is therefore protected by the First Amendment to the US Constitution. But city, state, and federal governments have enacted rules that govern protests, and violators can be arrested. For example, the right to protest does not extend to private property. In other words, protesters can gather in town parks or public squares, but if they wander onto the properties of businesses or home owners, they would be regarded as trespassers and therefore in violation of the law.

Many cities require protesters to obtain permits for demonstrations that are likely to restrict traffic flow on city streets or otherwise interrupt other people's lives. If the protest organizers want to march down the center of a busy street, for instance, they must get a permit. This also alerts police to the need to block traffic on that street until the protesters pass. This process ensures the freedom to exercise First Amendment rights in public spaces.

those individuals that are causing the violence or destruction and hold them accountable."[35]

Police Kneel in Support

Hancock was not the only big city mayor to side with the protesters. In Milwaukee, Wisconsin, Mayor Tom Barrett, who is White, marched with the protesters during a June 2 rally. "People have a right to be angry, people have a right to demand change and we need change," Barrett said. "People are upset, they're rightfully upset. They're angry. I'm angry at what I saw [in the Floyd arrest video]. We have to be a society where everyone is treated with respect."[36]

Moreover, during the protests of 2020, it was not unusual to see many police officers kneel down as the protesters marched past them, sending a signal to the demonstrators that they support their cause. Aleeia Abraham, who attended a demonstration in New York City on May 31, saw several officers kneel in support of the protesters. She welcomed the gesture but suggested the officers have to do more than kneel in support of the movement to end racial injustice. "That's great, it's a good sign, but what we're really looking for is action," she said. "I'll be even more impressed when we're not stepped on and gunned down. That's the moment I'm looking for."[37]

In some cases police officers actually joined the protests. Among them was Joseph Wysocki, chief of police in Camden, New Jersey, who marched alongside protesters on May 30—five days after Floyd's death. "Watching Floyd's murder unfold on video, every cop in the country is sick to their stomach," said Wysocki. "Good cops are hurt by what they saw. So I thought it was important to walk with the protesters."[38] During the march that day, the police chief carried a banner that read "Standing in Solidarity."

Meanwhile, at a May 30 protest in Flint Township, Michigan, protesters found themselves facing police in riot gear. With tensions escalating, Chris Swanson, the county sheriff, suddenly

stepped out of the ranks of the police officers facing the protesters. He took off his helmet and placed it on the ground, then he ordered the officers to put away their batons. "I want to make this a parade, not a protest,"[39] he told the crowd. The protest then resumed with Swanson marching alongside the demonstrators.

Tear Gas Employed by Police

But not all mayors, police chiefs, or rank-and-file officers were as sympathetic to the protesters in their cities. Some of the interactions between police and protesters turned ugly. In some cities, police resorted to tasers, tear gas, and pepper spray. They also used physical force, as happened on June 4 when seventy-five-year-old protester Martin Gugino was captured on cell phone video approaching police officers in Buffalo, New York. Suddenly, two Buffalo officers shoved Gugino out of their way. He fell to the ground, suffering a head injury. For several minutes other officers strode by the man as he lay bleeding on the ground, until he was finally assisted and transported to a nearby hospital. Days following the incident, the two officers who were alleged to have shoved Gugino, Robert McCabe and Aaron Torgalski, were suspended without pay and charged with criminally assaulting the protester. "The incident in Buffalo is wholly unjustified and utterly disgraceful," said New York governor Andrew Cuomo. "The protestors are truthful in their righteous indignation, and they have the right to protest, and they should not be abused, and there should not be undue force, and they shouldn't get hit with a baton for no reason, and, by the way, no self-respecting cop would defend any of that."[40]

Meanwhile, in Huntsville, Alabama, protests staged in late May and early June were broken up by police. Dozens of protesters were arrested. Leaders of the protests claimed the demonstrations were peaceful, and there was no need for police to step in. "There was nothing violent to occur, we knelt, we chanted, we did everything we had to,"[41] said a protester who identified herself as Madison.

But Huntsville police chief Mark McMurray said his department analyzed evidence it gathered before the protests were staged. He said the evidence suggested that outside agitators were planning to commit lootings, vandalism, and other violent acts. He said the department had received tips from sources among the demonstrators indicating that violence could break out on Huntsville streets. "This information we received caused us to make some very hard decisions," said McMurray. "But they had to be made to protect the citizens of Huntsville and the city."[42]

In breaking up the protests, police in Huntsville—as well as other cities—resorted to using tear gas to dispel the crowds. As the name suggests, tear gas is a substance that causes a stinging sensation in the eyes as well as burning sensations in the nose and mouth. Typically, the effects last for about thirty minutes, but people who suffer from respiratory disabilities—such as asthma—may find their lives endangered if they are subjected to a tear gas attack. A Black woman named Sam who participated in a protest in Atlanta, Georgia, was the victim of a tear gas attack. Sam said the protesters gathered in front of a city police station. At first, she said, the protest was peaceful—some of the police officers standing in front of the station knelt down in support of the protesters. But then one of the protesters tossed a firecracker into a group of police officers. The officers quickly donned helmets and other riot gear. Within seconds, Sam said, the officers tossed tear gas canisters into the crowd of protesters. Sam said the gas created a burning sensation in her eyes and throat. She said, "Every time you open your eyes it feels like there's lemon juice in them."[43]

In Huntsville, Mayor Tommy Battle defended the actions of the police in breaking up the demonstration. "Police were clear in their instructions and worked with the remaining protesters for more than an hour before using non-lethal irritants," Battle said. "The protesters had every opportunity to peacefully leave and they chose otherwise."[44]

> "Police were clear in their instructions and worked with the remaining protesters for more than an hour before using non-lethal irritants."[44]
>
> —Huntsville, Alabama, mayor Tommy Battle

Trump Denounces Demonstrations

Battle was one of many governmental leaders in the United States to show little tolerance for the protests, focusing more on the rallies that devolved into violence and vandalism than on the many peaceful demonstrations. On June 1 President Donald Trump participated in a conference call with the nation's fifty governors. He demanded that they take a harder line against protesters—urging them to call out National Guard troops to quell the violence. "You have to dominate, if you don't dominate you're wasting your time. They're going to run over you. You're going to look like a bunch of jerks. You have to dominate,"[45] the president told the governors.

Later that day, Trump spoke in the White House Rose Garden. He portrayed the violence and looting as acts of domestic terror and threatened to call out the military if city or state leaders failed to act. He said:

> We are ending the riots and lawlessness that has spread throughout our country. We will end it now. Today, I have strongly recommended to every governor to deploy the National Guard in sufficient numbers that we dominate the streets. Mayors and governors must establish an overwhelming law enforcement presence until the violence has been quelled.[46]

Shortly after his speech, military police used tear gas and flash grenades to clear peaceful protesters from a location outside the White House so that the president could be photographed holding a Bible while standing beside a boarded-up church.

Federal Officers Arrive in Portland

The resources Trump described in his White House Rose Garden speech would soon be deployed in Portland, Oregon, to quell demonstrations that erupted after Floyd's death. The protests in Portland took an ugly turn early on. On May 29, the second night of the protests, vandals damaged numerous government buildings as well as private businesses. Police stepped in that night and deployed tear gas to disperse the protesters, but over the course of the next few weeks, incidents of vandalism as well as looting continued to mark the Portland protests.

On July 1 more than one hundred federal officers, clad in riot gear and camouflage uniforms, trooped into town. Federal officials said the officers were deployed to protect the federal courthouse, which had already been vandalized. But the federal officers were also deployed in other parts of the city, far from any properties owned by the federal government. They used tear gas and pepper spray to quell the demonstrations in Portland.

Moreover, witnesses saw the federal officers take protesters into custody and force them into unmarked vans and other vehicles. In the early morning hours of July 17, two Portland men, Mark Pettibone and Conner O'Shea, decided to return to their homes after spending several hours protesting in front of the county courthouse. Both men recalled that the demonstration they attended had been relatively calm. Although tempers were raw, no one in the crowd committed acts of vandalism.

Pettibone and O'Shea were actually walking away from the demonstration when they saw an unmarked van stop nearby. Officers wearing camouflage uniforms jumped out of the van and grabbed people off the street, throwing them into the van. O'Shea ran from the scene, but Pettibone was caught. The officers pulled his hat over his eyes so he could not see. He was driven around for several minutes, along with several other protesters who had been arrested. Finally, the van came to a stop at the federal courthouse. The protesters were hustled out of the van and taken to jail cells. "It was basically a process of facing many walls and corners as they patted me down and took my picture and rummaged through my belongings,"[47] Pettibone said.

Pettibone said he was never told why he was arrested. The officers asked him if he wanted to give a statement. He declined and said he wished to speak with a lawyer. About ninety minutes later, he was released from custody. Critics reacted harshly to the treatment of the Portland protesters, particularly in cases where they were snatched off the streets and forced into unmarked vans. "Usually when we see people in unmarked cars forcibly grab someone off the street we call it kidnapping," said Jann Carson, an attorney for the American Civil Liberties Union. "The actions of the militarized federal officers are flat-out unconstitutional and will not go unanswered."[48]

Portland Mayor Tear-Gassed

As protesters filled the streets of Portland, Oregon, Mayor Ted Wheeler called out the city police to clear the streets. Portland police used tear gas to quell the demonstrations. But once federal agents showed up and started arresting peaceful protesters and tossing them into jail, Wheeler called on them to leave. On July 22, to show his support for the protesters, Wheeler joined them in a demonstration in front of the federal courthouse in Portland.

He quickly found himself facing a hostile crowd. Protesters complained that he had shown little regard for them by permitting city police to use tear gas to break up the protests. As Wheeler heard insults and calls for his resignation, federal officers surrounded the protesters. Suddenly, the federal officers hurled tear gas canisters toward the crowd of protesters. Wheeler was among the individuals who inhaled the tear gas, gaining firsthand knowledge of what the protesters went through when they were tear-gassed by city police under his leadership. "I'm not going to lie—it stings; it's hard to breathe," Wheeler said. "And I can tell you with 100 percent honesty, I saw nothing which provoked this response."

Quoted in Mike Baker, "Federal Agents Envelop Portland Protest, and City's Mayor, in Tear Gas," *New York Times*, July 23, 2020. www.nytimes.com.

Ken Cuccinelli, acting secretary of the US Department of Homeland Security, defended the use of the camouflaged officers and unmarked vehicles in making the arrests. He said:

I fully expect that as long as people continue to be violent and to destroy property that we will attempt to identify those folks. We will pick them up in front of the courthouse. If we spot them elsewhere, we will pick them up elsewhere. And if we have a question about somebody's identity . . . after questioning determines it isn't someone of interest, then they get released.[49]

Wall of Moms

Others who had been tear-gassed that week included numerous members of the Wall of Moms—a group of mothers both from Portland and surrounding suburbs.

Hundreds of women from this group poured onto Portland's streets to protest the use of federal officers and their tactics. Facing off against the federal officers, many of the women shouted, "Don't shoot your mother" and "Hands up, please don't shoot me." Jennie Vinson, a forty-three-year-old mother, said she was prompted to take part in the demonstrations because, during the last moments of his life, Floyd was recorded on the video calling out for his mother. "When you're a mom you have this primal urge to protect kids, and not just your kids, all kids," said Vinson, who helped organize the Wall of Moms demonstration. "To see a grown man reaching out and calling for his mother—I think that was a transformational moment for so many of us. It's like: What choice do we have but to do this?"[50]

Tensions finally eased in late July when officials from the US Department of Homeland Security agreed to withdraw the federal force. In its place, Oregon governor Kate Brown deployed members of the Oregon State Police. Travis Hampton, the superintendent of the Oregon State Police, promised that the state troopers would use a much gentler approach in overseeing the protests. "It is clear we cannot police our way out of this conflict," he said. "We are hoping that supplanting federal officers with troopers will lower the temperature a bit."[51]

During the spring and summer of 2020, as protests against racial injustice swept through America, the nation's political leaders displayed dramatically

> "To see a grown man reaching out and calling for his mother—I think that was a transformational moment for so many of us."[50]
>
> —Jennie Vinson, Wall of Moms protest organizer in Portland, Oregon

different attitudes toward the demonstrations. In places like Denver and Milwaukee, mayors marched with the protesters and promised to change the cultures of their police departments. But other political leaders, ranging from Huntsville mayor Tommy Battle to US president Donald Trump, took much harder lines, employing police to use strong-arm tactics to break up the protests. These examples show that Americans and their political leaders are hardly united on the issue of racial injustice.

Portland's protesters included the yellow-clad Wall of Moms. These chiefly White, suburban mothers responded to the death of George Floyd by taking to the streets and forming a protective barrier between federal agents and demonstrators.

CHAPTER FOUR

Have the Protests Led to Change?

As protesters took to the streets of Minneapolis following the death of George Floyd, the slogan "Defund the Police" was chanted over and over again. "We are going to dismantle the Minneapolis Police Department," said Jeremiah Ellison, an African American member of the Minneapolis City Council who participated in the protests. "And when we're done, we're not simply gonna glue it back together."[52]

Similar statements were made by protesters in other cities. In Los Angeles, New York City, Seattle, and other cities, many activists suggested that if police departments continued to abuse Black Americans as well as members of other minorities, the tax dollars that support those police departments should be cut off.

But to actually defund the police—for city and state governments to cut off all funding to police departments—would be, in the minds of many people, unthinkable. It would mean that when a crime is committed or an emergency occurs, residents would not be able to call on police for help. Robberies and burglaries, domestic violence, and even murder would have no consequences, and victims would have no recourse. Some say lawlessness would be pervasive—it would be as though American cities, small towns, and suburban communities had returned to the days of the Old West, when gun-toting cowboys protected themselves and their cattle from rustlers. "It is ridiculous to suggest we don't need law enforcement," says Tom Homan, a political commentator and former police officer. "A nation without law and order isn't a nation at all."[53]

"It is ridiculous to suggest we don't need law enforcement. A nation without law and order isn't a nation at all."[53]

—Tom Homan, political commentator and former police officer

Crisis Responders

In fact, many supporters of the Defund the Police movement do not want to totally disband their city and state police agencies. While they do favor cutting back their budgets, they would also cut back on their responsibilities. Rashawn Ray, a professor of sociology at the University of Maryland who has studied the causes of police violence, points out that nine out of ten incidents to which police are summoned are nonviolent episodes that probably do not require a police presence. Ray says:

> They respond to everything from potholes in the street to cats stuck up a tree. Police officers are also increasingly asked to complete paperwork and online forms. . . . It could be argued, however, that reducing officer workload would increase the likelihood of solving violent crimes. Police officers are overworked and overstressed. Focusing on menial tasks throughout the day is inefficient and a waste of taxpayer money.[54]

Ray argues that if police were relieved of the duty of resolving neighborhood quarrels or rescuing stray cats, their time could be better used for pursuing violent criminals. He cites national statistics compiled by the FBI that showed in 2017—the last year for which statistics are available—38 percent of murders, 66 percent of rapes, 70 percent of robberies, and 47 percent of aggravated assaults do not result in the arrests of perpetrators.

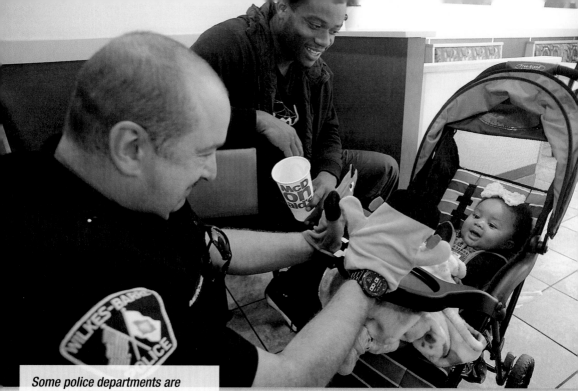

Some police departments are reforming their policies in response to growing tensions between law enforcement and the public. Changes include instituting minority sensitivity training and requiring more interaction between officers and members of the community they serve.

Under police department defunding plans, the money that would have gone into new weapons and new personnel would instead be spent on social programs to improve the lives of Black Americans and others so that it would be less likely that police would be called in to intervene in situations in which they are not really needed. Such programs would be aimed at reducing drug addiction in impoverished neighborhoods as well as homelessness and hunger. Funds would also be targeted toward providing treatment for mentally ill persons.

By the summer of 2020, some cities had taken the initial steps to defund their police departments. The Los Angeles City Council voted to strip $150 million out of the police department's $1.8 billion annual budget. City council members said they plan to reallocate the money into social services in an effort to improve the lives of Black citizens and others who live in impoverished communities. Moreover, some of the funds will be used to establish a new unit that would dispatch city "crisis responders" to nonviolent incidents where mediation, and not force, would be used to quell tempers. "We need to reimagine public safety in the 21st century," says Los Angeles City Council member Herb Wesson Jr. "One which reduces the need for armed police presence, especially when the situation does not necessarily require it."[55]

City council members in Seattle also approved a plan to cut the city's $400 million police budget by about $3 million. As in Los Angeles, Seattle plans to provide aid for homeless and drug-addicted people and establish a Department of Community Safety and Violence Prevention within the city government. The new department's crisis responders will be dispatched to the scenes of nonviolent confrontations or other incidents to resolve the disputes without the need to involve police.

> "We need to reimagine public safety in the 21st century. One which reduces the need for armed police presence, especially when the situation does not necessarily require it."[55]
>
> —Los Angeles City Council member Herb Wesson Jr.

Another strategy favored by reformers is not to defund the police but rather to dismantle and rebuild the departments. They point to the city of Camden, New Jersey, which—after years of charges of police abuse against Black citizens—rebuilt its police department in 2013. All police officers were fired and invited to reapply for their old jobs. Many were not rehired; instead, they were replaced with new officers as well as new leaders who emphasized nonviolent responses to minor incidents. Police officers were trained in de-escalation tactics. Sean Brown, a Camden resident and business owner, says he finds a much different attitude among police officers than he observed before the department was dismantled and rebuilt. Says Brown, "Every couple of months I get a call from an officer, who just asks me how is everything going in my neighborhood? Do I feel safe? Is there anything I want to tell them? Things are demonstrably different."[56]

Police Officers Face Criminal Charges

While many cities wrestled with how (or whether) to reorganize their police departments, cities where specific cases of police abuse occurred faced the prospect of arresting and prosecuting the officers. In Minneapolis, police officer Derek Chauvin was fired from the police department and charged with the murder of Floyd. If convicted, he could face a maximum penalty of forty years in prison. As of the fall of 2020, he was awaiting trial. The three other police officers who were charged with assisting Chauvin in detaining Floyd—Thomas Kiernan Lane, Alexander Kueng, and Tou Nmn Thao—were also fired from the Minneapolis police. The three former officers were charged with aiding and abetting murder. If convicted, each defendant could also face maximum penalties of forty years in prison.

Charges against the officers in the Floyd case were filed within a week of his death. This differed markedly from what took place in Louisville. The results of an investigation into the March 13 shooting death of Breonna Taylor were released on September 23—six months after she died. The outcome was also very different. Kentucky's attorney general announced a charge of wanton endangerment against one of the officers involved in the raid. That officer, Brett Hankison, was fired in June. The charge he faces involves allegations of recklessly firing into a neighbor's apartment. No charges were filed against the other two officers, who fired multiple shots including the one that killed Taylor. No one was charged with causing her death.

Prosecutors said the case presented thorny legal issues that made it difficult to charge the three officers. The no-knock warrant gave them permission to burst into Taylor's apartment. Attorneys for Hankison and the other officers maintained that when Taylor's boyfriend drew his gun on the police, they were within their rights to fire their weapons. Walker has said he and Taylor feared her ex-boyfriend was trying to break into the apartment, which is why he shot at the intruders.

Statues Honoring Slaveholders Come Down

Throughout 2020 many protesters congregated in parks where statues of eighteenth- and nineteenth-century heroes have stood for years. But these heroes were also slave owners. Protesters demanded removal of the statues. In many cases they vandalized the statues or knocked them down on their own. Under pressure from the protesters, many city governments did remove the statues. In Richmond, Virginia, for example, the city government removed statues of General Stonewall Jackson as well as other leaders of the Confederate army. Said Richmond mayor Levar Stoney, "Those statues stood high for over 100 years for a reason, and it was to intimidate and to show black and brown people in this city who was in charge. I think the healing can now begin in the city of Richmond."

Quoted in Kenneth Garger, "City of Richmond Removes Statue of Confederate General Stonewall Jackson," *New York Post*, July 1, 2020. https://nypost.com.

Prosecutors faced enormous pressure from protesters and others to bring charges against the Louisville police officers. After the single charge against Hankison was announced protesters poured into the streets of Louisville and other cities. They called for further investigation and charges against the officers responsible for Taylor's death. Among the people making these demands was National Basketball Association (NBA) superstar LeBron James. "We want the cops arrested who committed that crime," says James. "I want her family to know and I want the state of Kentucky to know that . . . we want justice."[57] Other NBA players made their feelings known during the 2020 season. Many players had the slogan "Say Her Name"—a reference to Taylor—sewn into the backs of their jerseys.

The FBI said it was still investigating the case and did not rule out the possibility that federal charges could be

> "I want [Breonna Taylor's] family to know and I want the state of Kentucky to know that . . . we want justice."[57]
>
> —NBA star LeBron James

filed against all three officers who burst into Taylor's apartment. In the meantime, Louisville officials agreed to settle a civil lawsuit brought against the police by Taylor's family. Under the terms of the settlement, the city did not have to acknowledge wrongdoing by the police officers involved in the incident; nevertheless, the city agreed to pay Taylor's family $12 million as well as enact reforms in the police department. Among those reforms are programs to encourage police officers to live in neighborhoods populated largely by Blacks. Officers will also be required to volunteer for community improvement projects in low-income neighborhoods.

Banning Chokeholds and No-Knock Warrants

While police departments faced budget cuts as well as the arrests of some of their officers, city and state governments throughout America acted to curtail many of the methods used in arrests. After the video of Chauvin emerged showing him kneeling on the neck of Floyd, dozens of police departments banned the use of any type of chokehold by officers. Speaking at Floyd's funeral on June 9, Houston mayor Sylvester Turner said, "The city attorney is drafting an executive order, an order that I will sign when I get back to city hall, and what that order will say is that in this city, we will ban chokeholds and strangleholds."[58] Moreover, many state legislatures took action in 2020 to ban chokeholds for every police department in their state, and a bill was introduced in Congress to enact a national ban on the tactic.

The use of the no-knock warrant, which ultimately led to the death of Taylor, was also banned by many cities. In Louisville the city council unanimously passed a measure it titled Breonna's Law, eliminating no-knock warrants from the arsenal of measures police can employ against suspects. Taylor's mother, Tamika Palmer, pointed out that as an emergency medical technician, her daughter helped save many lives on the ambulance crews on which she served. "Breonna, that's all she wanted to do was to save lives," says Palmer. "So with this law, she will be able to continue to do that. So we're grateful for that."[59]

A Downside of Defunding the Police

The Defund the Police movement seeks to divert money from police departments to social programs that would aid Black citizens, but cutting police budgets may also have a detrimental effect on the Black community. It would mean there would be less money to hire new police officers, which means there would be fewer opportunities for Black candidates for those jobs. "If you want diversity, if you want quality candidates, you have to go out and find those candidates. That costs money," says Matt Cobb, who oversees recruiting for the Topeka, Kansas, Police Department. "If we don't have the money to recruit people, then how do we fix the things people have said about us?"

Moreover, according to the Police Executive Research Forum (PERF), a Washington, DC–based group that studies trends in law enforcement, the average age of American police officers has been rising in recent years. By 2025, a PERF study says, some 25 percent of American police officers will be eligible for retirement. This means that if many communities adopt Defund the Police measures, there will be many vacancies in those departments but a lack of funds to pay new recruits, including Black recruits.

Quoted in Jeff Mordock, "Misguided 'Defund Police' Movement Undercuts Effort to Change Culture, Experts Warn," *Washington Times*, July 1, 2020. www.washingtontimes.com.

Other cities banned no-knock warrants as well. Among them were San Antonio, Texas; South Fulton, Georgia; and Orlando, Florida. By the late summer of 2020, dozens of other city and state governments were preparing to act on similar measures to ban no-knock warrants. In communities where no-knock warrants have been banned, it means police officers who obtain search warrants for homes or businesses must first announce to the occupants that they have obtained a court-issued warrant that gives them permission to search the premises for illegal drugs, weapons, or similar evidence of criminal conduct.

America Reassesses Its Treatment of Minorities

The protests sparked by the deaths of Floyd and Taylor soon moved beyond the issue of police abuse. Many protest leaders said police abuse of Black Americans is but one example of how racial injustice has been an accepted part of American culture. Indeed, the protests prompted leaders of many institutions of American society to look inward and reassess how they have treated not only Black Americans but other minority groups as well. For example, for years many Native Americans have called for the Washington Redskins of the National Football League (NFL) to change the team's name, insisting that the term *redskin* is a racial slur. And for years Redskins owner Daniel Snyder resisted these demands, claiming the team enjoyed a long tradition dating back to the 1930s of playing under that name. But in 2020 Snyder announced that the team would finally drop the name and seek another name. (At the start of the 2020 NFL season, the team had not yet adopted a new name; it was being called the "Washington football team" for the time being.)

Other organizations made similar changes. Quaker Oats, a company that makes many breakfast goods, announced in June 2020 that it would rename its brands of Aunt Jemima syrup and pancake mix. For decades the brand, which is more than 130 years old, featured a Black woman dressed in the work clothes of a housekeeper—which critics insisted perpetrated a racial stereotype. "We recognize Aunt Jemima's origins are based on a racial stereotype," says Kristin Kroepfl, vice president of Quaker Oats. "As we work to make progress toward racial equality through several initiatives, we also must take a hard look at our portfolio of brands and ensure they reflect our values and meet our consumers' expectations."[60] Similarly, Mars Inc., the company that owns the Uncle Ben's brand of rice products, said it would also seek a new name for the brand. On the company's packaging, Uncle Ben is portrayed as an aging, white-haired Black man wearing a bow tie, which critics charge is a racial stereotype depicting a servant.

The streaming service HBO Max announced it would no longer offer the 1939 film *Gone with the Wind* to viewers. The film portrays life on a Southern plantation during the Civil War. Long regarded as a film classic—the movie won eight Academy Awards—it has nevertheless been criticized of late for its stereotypical portrayal of Black slaves. Says Hollywood screenwriter John Ridley, who supported the removal of the film from the streaming service, "It is a film that, when it is not ignoring the horrors of slavery, pauses only to perpetuate some of the most painful stereotypes of people of color."[61]

Continuing Use of Deadly Force

Changes like these were prompted by the widespread protests that commenced after George Floyd's death. And yet, despite these protests and the national attention that focused on how police treat Black suspects, in many cases police have not curtailed their use of deadly force even when it seems unwarranted. On August 23, 2020, police in Kenosha, Wisconsin, were called by a woman who reported that her boyfriend was at her home and acting unruly. Police arrived to find Jacob Blake, age twenty-nine, at the home. Police followed Blake to his car, which held his three sons. As Blake resisted attempts to place him under arrest and attempted to enter the car, in which he claimed to have a weapon, he was shot in the back seven times by a Kenosha police officer. The shooting left Blake paralyzed.

Angry protests broke out in Kenosha within hours and soon spread across the nation. On August 27, players in the NBA and other professional sports leagues refused to participate in games to show their support for Blake and other victims of racial injustice. Said a statement issued by the players for the Milwaukee Bucks of the NBA, "When we take the court and represent Milwaukee and Wisconsin, we are expected to play at a high level, give maximum effort and hold each other accountable. We hold ourselves to that standard, and in this moment, we are demanding the same from our lawmakers and law enforcement. We are calling for justice for Jacob Blake."[62]

Although many segments of US society have begun to look at their own beliefs and actions in perpetuating racial injustice, the challenges are huge. Black Americans are still being killed by police. They are still being subjected to treatment that most other Americans do not normally experience. But the uproar and protests that followed the deaths of Floyd, Taylor, and other victims have made it abundantly clear that Black Americans, and many others as well, will no longer tolerate these actions and attitudes.

Introduction: The Chokehold

1. Quoted in Omar Jimenez, "New Police Body Camera Footage Reveals George Floyd's Last Words Were 'I Can't Breathe,'" CNN, July 15, 2020. www.cnn.com.
2. Donald T. Reay and John W. Eisele, "Death from Law Enforcement Neck Holds," *American Journal of Forensic Medicine and Pathology*, September 1982, p. 258.
3. Eileen Rivers, "Video of George Floyd Pinned by Minneapolis Cops Is Shocking but Not Surprising," *USA Today*, May 27, 2020. www.usatoday.com.

Chapter One: Enduring Decades of Injustice

4. Quoted in Holly Bailey et al., "'It's a Blue-Soaked Anger': Amid Protests, African Americans Feel a Private Grief," *Washington Post*, May 31, 2020. www.washingtonpost.com.
5. Quoted in Bailey et al., "'It's a Blue-Soaked Anger.'"
6. Adrienne Green, "The Cost of Balancing Academia and Racism," *The Atlantic*, January 21, 2016. www.theatlantic.com.
7. Lynne Peeples, "What the Data Say About Police Shootings," *Nature*, September 4, 2019. www.nature.com.
8. Frank Edwards et al., "Risk of Being Killed by Police Use of Force in the United States by Age, Race-Ethnicity, and Sex," *Proceedings of the National Academy of Sciences*, August 20, 2019. www.pnas.org.
9. Quoted in Wenei Philimon, "Not Just George Floyd: Police Departments Have 400-Year History of Racism," *USA Today*, June 7, 2020. www.usatoday.com.
10. Quoted in Simone Weichselbaum, "One Roadblock to Police Reform: Veteran Officers Who Train Recruits," NBC News, July 22, 2020. www.nbcnews.com.
11. Quoted in Sam Sanders, "A Black Mother Reflects on Giving Her 3 Sons 'the Talk' . . . Again and Again," National Public Radio, June 28, 2020. www.npr.org.

12. Quoted in Kanya Bennett, "Say Her Name: Recognizing Police Brutality Against Black Women," American Civil Liberties Union, June 14, 2018. www.aclu.org.
13. Arwa Mahdawi, "We Must Keep Fighting for Justice for Breonna Taylor. We Must Keep Saying Her Name," *The Guardian* (Manchester, UK), June 6, 2020. www.theguardian.com.
14. Wesley Lowery, "Black Lives Matter: Birth of a Movement," *The Guardian* (Manchester, UK), January 17, 2017. www.theguardian.com.
15. Quoted in Lowery, "Black Lives Matter."
16. Quoted in Julie Bosman and Joseph Goldstein, "Timeline for a Body: 4 Hours in the Middle of a Ferguson Street," *New York Times*, August 23, 2014. www.nytimes.com.
17. Quoted in Monica Davey and Julie Bosman, "Protests Flare After Ferguson Police Officer Is Not Indicted," *New York Times*, November 24, 2014. www.nytimes.com.

Chapter Two: Protests Sweep Across America

18. Quoted in Paul DeBenedetto et al., "Rappers, Elected Officials Join Family of George Floyd in Downtown March," Houston Public Media, June 2, 2020. www.houstonpublicmedia.org.
19. Quoted in DeBenedetto et al., "Rappers, Elected Officials Join Family of George Floyd in Downtown March."
20. Quoted in DeBenedetto et al., "Rappers, Elected Officials Join Family of George Floyd in Downtown March."
21. Quoted in Ernest Scheyder, "George Floyd, a 'Gentle Giant,' Remembered in Hometown Houston March," Reuters, June 2, 2020. www.reuters.com.
22. Quoted in DeBenedetto et al., "Rappers, Elected Officials Join Family of George Floyd in Downtown March."
23. Quoted in Nikita Stewart, "Black Activists Wonder: Is Protesting Just Trendy for White People?," *New York Times*, June 26, 2020. www.nytimes.com.
24. Quoted in Stewart, "Black Activists Wonder."
25. Quoted in Bruce Schreiner, "Kentucky: Elderly Whites Protest for Slain Black Woman." Associated Press, August 20, 2020. apnews.com.
26. Quoted in Claudia Vargas, "Most Looters Are Young Philadelphians Not Associated with the Protests, DA Says," NBC 10, June 1, 2020. www.nbcphiladelphia.com.

27. Quoted in Robert Moran, "Philly Police Commissioner Danielle Outlaw Condemns Death of George Floyd in Minneapolis Police Custody," *Philadelphia Inquirer*, May 28, 2020. www.inquirer.com.

28. Quoted in Rudy Chinchilla and David Chang, "Looting, Violence Drown Out Peaceful George Floyd Protests in Philadelphia," NBC 10, June 1, 2020. www.nbcphiladelphia.com.

29. Quoted in Chinchilla and Chang, "Looting, Violence Drown Out Peaceful George Floyd Protests in Philadelphia."

30. Quoted in Bob Keeler, "Hundreds Take Part in Peaceful Souderton Protest March," *Souderton (PA) Independent*, June 5, 2020. www.montgomerynews.com.

31. Quoted in Keeler, "Hundreds Take Part in Peaceful Souderton Protest March."

32. Quoted in Adrian Florido and Marisa Penaloza, "As Nation Reckons with Race, Poll Finds White Americans Least Engaged," National Public Radio, August 27, 2020. www.npr.org.

33. Quoted in Alec Rich, "Massive Turnout for Eisenhower Park Back the Blue Rally," *Long Island (NY) Press*, July 26, 2020. www.longislandpress.com.

Chapter Three: Governments Respond to the Protests

34. Quoted in CBS 4, "'I'm Proud of the Demonstrations': Denver Mayor Michael Hancock Marches with Protesters Downtown," June 3, 2020. https://denver.cbslocal.com.

35. Quoted in Front Porch, "Q&A with Chief Pazen," July 1, 2020. https://frontporchne.com.

36. Quoted in Ricardo Torres, "'We All Want to Be Safe': Huge March from Bay View Was Peaceful for Most of Tuesday, Included Moments of Unity," *Milwaukee (WI) Journal Sentinel*, June 3, 2020. www.jsonline.com.

37. Quoted in Hannah Knowles and Isaac Stanley-Becker, "Some Officers March and Kneel with Protesters, Creating Dissonant Images on Fraught Weekend of Uprisings," *Washington Post*, June 1, 2020. www.washingtonpost.com.

38. Quoted in K.C. Baker, "Police Join Protesters in Marches Across the Country: 'Good Cops Are Sick to Their Stomachs,'" *People*, June 1, 2020. https://people.com.

39. Quoted in Baker, "Police Join Protesters in Marches Across the Country."
40. Quoted in Nick Reisman, "Cuomo Condemns Buffalo Police Appearing to Shove Protester to the Ground," Spectrum News, June 5, 2020. https://spectrumlocalnews.com.
41. Quoted in WBRC 6, "Downtown Huntsville Protest Ends with Riot Gas, Arrests," June 3, 2020. www.wbrc.com.
42. Quoted in Caroline Klapp, "Huntsville Police Chief Spends Hours Explaining Response to Protests," WAFF 48, June 18, 2020. www.waff.com.
43. Quoted in Ryan Prior, "Tear Gas: Prepare for What to Do If You're Exposed," CNN, June 3, 2020. www.cnn.com.
44. Quoted in Paul Gattis, "Huntsville Mayor Tommy Battle Defends Police Use of Tear Gas," AL.com, June 4, 2020. www.al.com.
45. Quoted in CNN, "President Trump's Call with US Governors over Protests," June 1, 2020. www.cnn.com.
46. White House, "Statement by the President," June 1, 2020. www.whitehouse.gov.
47. Quoted in Jonathan Levinson et al., "Federal Officers Use Unmarked Vehicles to Grab People in Portland, DHS Confirms," National Public Radio, July 17, 2020. www.npr.org.
48. Quoted in Associated Press, "Portland Mayor Demands Trump Remove Federal Agents from City," The Guardian (Manchester, UK), July 19, 2020. www.theguardian.com.
49. Quoted in Levinson et al., "Federal Officers Use Unmarked Vehicles to Grab People in Portland, DHS Confirms."
50. Quoted in Marissa J. Lang, "'What Choice Do We Have?' Portland's 'Wall of Moms' Faces Off with Federal Officers at Tense Protests," Washington Post, July 22, 2020. www.washingtonpost.com.
51. Quoted in Noelle Crombie, "Oregon State Police Take Over Portland Protest Duty: 'We Are Hoping for the Best but Planning for the Worst,'" The Oregonian (Portland, OR), July 30, 2020. www.oregonlive.com.

Chapter Four: Have the Protests Led to Change?

52. Quoted in Michael Balsamo, "When Protesters Demand 'Defund the Police' at George Floyd Demonstrations, What Does

It Mean?," *Chicago Tribune*, June 7, 2020. www.chicago tribune.com.

53. Tom Homan, "A Nation Without Police—If Dems Get Their Way, This Is How Our Communities Will Suffer," Fox News, June 10, 2020. www.foxnews.com.

54. Rashawn Ray, "What Does 'Defund the Police' Mean and Does It Have Merit?," Brookings Institution, June 19, 2020. www.brookings.edu.

55. Quoted in Saba Hamedy and Topher Gauk-Roger, "Los Angeles City Council Moves Forward with Plan to Replace Police Officers with Community-Based Responders for Nonviolent Calls," CNN, June 30, 2020. www.cnn.com.

56. Quoted in Katherine Landergan, "The City That Really Did Abolish the Police," *Politico*, June 12, 2020. www.politico.com.

57. Quoted in Melissa Rohlin, "LeBron James Delivers Passionate Comments About Breonna Taylor and the Need for Change," *Sports Illustrated*, July 23, 2020. www.si.com.

58. Quoted in ABC 13, "Mayor Turner to Sign Executive Order Banning Use of Chokeholds in Houston," June 9, 2020. https://abc13.com.

59. Quoted in Barbara Campbell, "No-Knock Warrants Banned in Louisville in Law Named for Breonna Taylor," National Public Radio, June 11, 2020. www.npr.org.

60. Quoted in Ben Kesslen, "Aunt Jemima Brand to Change Name, Remove Image That Quaker Says Is 'Based on a Racial Stereotype,'" NBC News, June 17, 2020. www.nbcnews.com.

61. Quoted in Abid Rahman, "HBO Max Removes Civil War Epic 'Gone with the Wind,'" *Hollywood Reporter*, June 9, 2020. www.hollywoodreporter.com.

62. Quoted in BBC, "More US Sports Events Postponed in Protest at Jacob Blake Shooting," August 27, 2020. www.bbc.com.

ORGANIZATIONS AND WEBSITES

Act for America, Back the Blue
www.actforamerica.org/activism/back-the-blue

The Washington, DC–based group Act for America established this website to document its efforts to organize Back the Blue demonstrations. Visitors to the group's website can find photos of Back the Blue demonstrations as well as social media links to connect with the group's mission.

American Civil Liberties Union (ACLU), Racial Justice
www.aclu.org/issues/racial-justice

The ACLU maintains this website to document its campaign to defend victims of racial injustice. By accessing the link for Court Cases, visitors can find information on how the ACLU has challenged government officials and others suspected of racial injustice.

Black Lives Matter
https://blacklivesmatter.com

Founded after the 2014 death of Michael Brown, Black Lives Matter has grown into a national organization dedicated to ending police violence against Blacks. Visitors to the group's website can find contact information for the sixteen regional chapters as well as news about the numerous rallies and protests organized by the group.

Centers for Disease Control and Prevention, Facts About Riot Control Agents
https://emergency.cdc.gov/agent/riotcontrol/factsheet.asp

The federal government's chief health monitoring agency provides facts about weapons such as tear gas and pepper spray used by police to quell unruly protesters. The website outlines the physical symptoms endured by victims if they are exposed to the substances as well as the possible long-term consequences of exposure.

Mapping Police Violence
https://mappingpoliceviolence.org

Organized by three data scientists, the website maintained by this group tracks police violence against Black citizens. By accessing the National Trends link, visitors can find information on violent methods of arrest perpetrated by individual police departments in the United States as well as the racial breakdown of suspects who have been shot by police officers.

US Department of Justice, Law Enforcement Misconduct
www.justice.gov/crt/law-enforcement-misconduct

The website examines federal laws that govern how criminal suspects are to be treated by the police. Specifically, the website outlines a 1948 law adopted by Congress that forbids police officers to deprive criminal suspects of their rights, including using unnecessary force in detaining them.

FOR FURTHER RESEARCH

Books

Paul Butler, *Chokehold: Policing Black Men*. New York: New Press, 2018.

Shaun King, *Make Change: How to Fight Injustice, Dismantle Systemic Oppression, and Own Our Future*. New York: Houghton Mifflin Harcourt, 2020.

Christopher Lebron, *The Making of Black Lives Matter: A Brief History of an Idea*. New York: Oxford University Press, 2018.

Hal Marcovitz, *Black in America*. San Diego, CA: ReferencePoint, 2020.

Internet Sources

Frank Edwards et al., "Risk of Being Killed by Police Use of Force in the United States by Age, Race-Ethnicity, and Sex," *Proceedings of the National Academy of Sciences*, August 20, 2019. www.pnas.org.

Wesley Lowery, "Black Lives Matter: Birth of a Movement," *The Guardian* (Manchester, UK), January 17, 2017. www.theguardian.com.

Lynne Peeples, "What the Data Say About Police Shootings," *Nature*, September 4, 2019. www.nature.com.

Rashawn Ray, "What Does 'Defund the Police' Mean and Does It Have Merit?," Brookings Institution, June 19, 2020. www.brookings.edu.

Donald T. Reay and John W. Eisele, "Death from Law Enforcement Neck Holds," *American Journal of Forensic Medicine and Pathology*, September 1982. www.charlydmiller.com.

Bryan Washington, "A Peaceful Protest, Cut Short by Police, in Houston with George Floyd's Family," *New Yorker*, June 4, 2020. www.newyorker.com.

INDEX